WITH ALCOHOL anything IS POPSICLE

HarperCollins*Publishers*

WITH ALCOHOL anything IS POPSICLE

60 Frozen Cocktails

JASSY DAVIS

HarperCollinsPublishers
1 London Bridge Street
London SE1 9GF

www.harpercollins.co.uk

First published by HarperCollins*Publishers* 2020

1 3 5 7 9 10 8 6 4 2

© HarperCollins*Publishers* 2020

Text by Jassy Davis
Images from Shutterstock
Design by Louise Evans

Jassy Davis asserts the moral right to be identified as the author of this work

A catalogue record of this book is available from the British Library

ISBN 978-0-00-838235-3

Printed and bound in Latvia by PNB Print Ltd.

MIX
Paper from
responsible sources
FSC™ C007454

FSC
www.fsc.org

This book is produced from independently certified FSC™ paper to ensure
responsible forest management.

For more information visit: www.harpercollins.co.uk/green

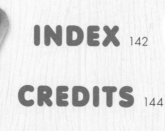

INTRODUCTION

ONCE UPON A TIME IN AMERICA...

... on one cold night, a boy called Frank Epperson made himself a drink and then forgot to drink it. It was 1905 and he was 11 years old, living in California, and too busy playing to remember to finish the drink he'd mixed himself. Back then, soft drinks were made simply by stirring a flavoured powder into water. Frank abandoned his half-drunk glass with the wooden stick still in it and left it on the porch, only remembering about it the next morning. When he picked it up he discovered that the drink had frozen solid. Somehow Frank managed to ease the ice out of the glass, using the stick as a handle, and that day he became the first person to ever lick an ice lolly.

Frank carried on making ice lollies for his friends, but more as a hobby or side line than as a job. It wasn't until he served up a tray of these ice pops at a local fireman's ball in 1922 and saw the sensation they caused that he thought there could be money to be made in these frozen treats.

He started off selling ice pops around his neighbourhood, calling them 'Eppsicles' – a portmanteau blending of his surname and the word icicle. His kids weren't fans of this branding; they'd already come up with their own name: Pop's 'Sicles. Deploying the kind of campaigning that only determined children can manage, they eventually persuaded him to change the name and Epperson set up America's first popsicle stand at the Neptune Beach amusement park on San Francisco Bay in 1923.

It didn't take long for the rest of the country to demand to know where their ice pops were, so Popsicle Corporation concessions opened in amusement parks and beaches across the USA. People loved them. One stand at Coney Island sold 8,000 Popsicles in just one day.

In June 1924, Frank applied for a patent for his Popsicle process. But, a few months later, and in need of money, he sold his patent to the Joe Lowe Corporation. If Popsicles had been popular when Epperson was making them, under Joe Lowe they were a national craze.

Even the Depression couldn't slow Popsicles down.

To keep these lollies affordable, Lowe came up with the two-handled Popsicle, a 5-cents ice pop that two kids could share.

But it wasn't all smiles in the ice lolly world. Epperson may have patented his icy invention, but he hadn't been the only one selling ices on a stick in the 1920s. In 1922 Harry Burt of Youngstown, Ohio, had patented the manufacturing process for chocolate-covered ice cream bars on a stick. He called them Good Humor bars and sold them from a fleet of ice-cream trucks. While in Texas in 1925, the M-B Ise Kream Company launched a range of fruit-flavoured Frozen Suckers on sticks. The advertising campaign called them 'the greatest treat you ever tasted' – and from the way they sold, it seems like the public agreed.

From 1924 to 1929, these three companies – and a few other ice-pop pedallers – tussled with each other through the courts, suing and countersuing over who had the legal right to make and sell ice pops. A wary truce was eventually called, with Good Humor retaining the right to sell 'ice creams, ice custards, and the like', while Popsicle held sway over 'flavoured syrup, water ice, or sherbet frozen on a stick'. M-B Ise Kream's suppliers, Citrus Products, became co-agents for Popsicle with the Joe Lowe Corporation, and for a while people could buy Popsicle-Frozen Suckers until the name was shortened again, back to Popsicle.

There were a few more legal skirmishes over the years – especially when Popsicle tested the water by launching a Milk Popsicle in 1932. These days peace is guaranteed, as Unilever owns both the Good Humor and Popsicle® brands, so there's no infighting allowed. And there's none needed either, when two billion Popsicles® are sold every year.

MEANWHILE, IN MEXICO

If you want to buy an ice lolly in Mexico, you go to La Michoacana. There are 15,000 of these pink-striped shops dotted across Mexico, each one brimming with jewel-bright *paletas* (the name translates as 'trowel' or 'little shovel'). These shops are not quite a chain, more an informal network of franchises owned by families who have a direct or indirect connection to one place: Tocumbo, a rural town in Mexico's Midwest. It's the little town that gave Mexico its taste for ice pops.

In 1946 two men waved goodbye to Tocumbo and set off for the bright lights of Mexico City. They were Ignacio Alcázar and Agustín Andrade and they both had the same dream: to set up a *paletería* selling fresh *paletas de agua* (water ices) and *paletas de leche* (milk ices). But to achieve it, they needed a neighbourhood where people had the spare change to treat themselves to a *paleta*.

In Mexico City they both set up ice-pop shops and they both thrived. The handmade *paletas*, made fresh every day, drew in the crowds. Ignacio's brother Luis joined him and they opened up more *paletarías*. It wasn't long until their friends and families back home got to hear about their success, and so a few more Tocumbo townsfolk moved to Mexico City and set up their own *paletarías* using the La Michoacana name. More Mexicans from home followed them, and the trickle of people became a flood. When every neighbourhood in Mexico City had a La Michoacana or two, the *paleteros* (paleta sellers) expanded their businesses out of the city until every major town in Mexico had their own *paletería*, all with a historic tie to Tocumbo.

These days Tocumbo celebrates the success of its *paleteros* with a week-long festival. Held in December, the *Feria de la Paleta* features a parade, sports events, funfairs, music and, of course, plenty of *paletas*.

A LITTLE WHILE LATER IN BRITAIN...

Ice pops arrived in Britain in the 1950s, just as food rationing was coming to an end. The first ice lollies to launch were simple, fruit-based treats. There was the Orange Maid, an orange juice 'drink on a stick', and the Mivvi, a vanilla ice-cream block coated in strawberry ice. As the years passed and the staid fifties segued into the swinging sixties, lollies started to get interesting.

The two major ice-lolly companies, Wall's and Lyons Maid, noticed the popularity of children's TV and began to develop lollies targeted at kids with TV tie-ins. Zoom, a layered lemon, lime and strawberry lolly shaped like a rocket, was launched in 1963 as a tie-in to Gerry Anderson's puppet show, Fireball XL5. Collect enough wrappers and you could send off for a model of the Fireball XL5 spaceship; while three Sea Jet lolly wrappers and a postal order for six shillings got you a model of Troy Tempest's Stingray.

In 1967, imagining girls were feeling left out with all these rocket- and submarine-themed lollies, Lyons Maid launched the FAB. A strawberry ice topped with vanilla ice cream and dipped in chocolate and hundreds and thousands, it was advertised by Thunderbirds' Lady Penelope.

Throughout the sixties and seventies, dozens of ice lollies linked with TV shows and movies were launched. There were the fruit-flavoured Mr Men lollies, Star Wars lollies, King Kong lollies and even Dalek Death Ray lollies (chocolate and mint).

Kids with an appetite for ice lollies were well served, but what about the grown-ups?

Lyons Maid had dipped their toe in the more sophisticated end of the lolly market in 1963 with the Pick of the Pops, a coffee-and-Advocaat-flavoured ice pop dipped in chocolate and biscuit pieces. However, it seems it didn't take off and alcohol, as an ingredient or flavouring, didn't feature much again until the eighties, when a new drinks craze caught the attention of Britain's ice-lolly manufacturers.

Cocktails had fallen out of fashion in the UK (too old-fashioned and boring) but a new wave of sticky sweet, neon-bright mixed drinks from the US had piqued people's interest. All of a sudden cocktails were fun, fab and glamorous. A nightclub without a Woo Woo or Fuzzy Navel on its menu was no nightclub at all.

But not everywhere had a barman capable of shaking up a Singapore Sling. How to bring that big city buzz into everyone's life? Enter Lyons Maid with their range of Cocktails on a Stick. Launched in 1984, they came in three flavours: Piña Colada, Tequila Sunrise and Brandy Alexander, and they promised a splash of rum, tequila or brandy, respectively, in every lolly. Britain's freezers had never been more stylish.

The fashion for boozy ice lollies didn't last, alas, so manufacturers began to focus on premium ice creams instead. In around 2008, gourmet ice-pop trucks and pushcarts began to appear in America, often opened by people who had tried *paletas* in Mexico and been knocked over by the freshness and quality of these handmade treats. By 2013 the carts and trucks had become stores and bars, and alcoholic ice pops had started appearing on their menus. The 'poptail' concept spread to the internet and it didn't take long for ice-lolly fans in Britain to think, once again, about how much they liked a splash of booze in their frozen treats.

POPS launched the world's first Champagne ice lolly in June 2014 with a glittering party in London. Company founders James Rae and Harry Clarke had come up with the idea while on holiday in Majorca, realising that there might be a market for something that was cooling but also a little boozy. Made with 37% Champagne, their push-up ice freezies were a sensation – especially on social media.

In 2015 the upper crust department store Fortnum & Mason launched their own range of Blanc de Blanc Champagne ice pops. It wasn't long before mass-market retailers got in on the act, offering Buck's Fizz, Cosmopolitan, gin and tonic and Bellini ice lollies to customers who were glad to find a fun way to cool down in the summer heatwave.

The concept caught on and boozy ice-lolly companies began to pop up around the world, tailoring the trend to local tastes. In South Africa, you will find ice pops made with blends of the country's famous wines, while Australia's booze-infused push-up pops mix classic cocktails with fresh fruits. American poptails have a whacking 10% ABV each, and in India the trendiest restobars serve boozy ice pops as part of their brunch menus.

Wherever you are in the world, you can be sure of just one thing: **when it comes to ice pops, they're no longer just for kids**.

THE LOLLY LOWDOWN

Making your own ice lollies is easier than you think. You don't need much in the way of special equipment, the ingredients are pretty budget-friendly, and they normally don't take more than 10 minutes to make (plus freezing time, of course).

The recipes in this book are simple to follow and designed so that you can jump straight in without any prior knowledge, so you can skip this section if you like. But if you want to be a bit of a nerd about getting your ice lollies just right, here are some things to remember.

Texture

Unlike ice creams and sorbets, ice pops are not churned, so they have a crisp, icy texture that melts in your mouth. Even those made with a dairy mix will have a firm, biteable texture. But you don't want your ice lollies to be too crunchy; the faster you freeze them, the smoother the texture will be. This is down to the size of the ice crystals that form while the lolly freezes.

A slow freeze creates big ice crystals, and sometimes these clump together as the lolly sets, creating a hard, bland middle while all the flavour and sweetness is pushed out to the edge of the ice pop. To keep your lollies smooth and evenly flavoured, make sure the mixture is cool when you freeze it and set your freezer to its lowest temperature or turn on the flash freeze feature. The bottom of your freezer is normally the coldest part, with the back of the bottom shelf or drawer the very coldest. Freeze your ice pops there – and don't keep opening the door to check on them while they freeze. As the saying goes, a watched lolly never freezes. Or, at least, it doesn't freeze that well.

One other thing that will affect the texture of your ice lolly is adding alcohol. Alcohol has a lower freezing point than syrups, fruit juices and dairy, and your kitchen freezer is unlikely to hit it. Ice pops made with alcohol will have a softer texture than liquor-free versions. Boozy poptails also melt faster, so be ready to be dripped on if you're not a quick eater.

Flavour

The freezing process can have a funny effect on flavours – some become stronger, some are diminished. One flavour that fades in the freezer is sweetness, which is why you need a surprising amount of sugar to make a truly sweet ice lolly. If you want to get that sugary hit, the mixture should taste sweeter than seems sensible in its liquid form. Once it's frozen, that sweetness will mellow out.

Spices, on the other hand, tend to taste stronger when they're frozen. If you're infusing a simple syrup with spices (see page 19 for the how-to), don't add too many and don't let the flavours infuse for too long.

Another flavour that gets dialled up during freezing is alcohol. Whether it's the sharp heat of vodka, the earthiness of tequila or the botanical richness of gin, you will taste it quite strongly in your finished ice pops. You might think that the orange juice and sugar syrup will hide the roughness of the cheap bottle of vodka leftover from last night's party, but it really won't. If you wouldn't drink it from a glass, don't freeze it onto a stick.

When it comes to the fresh ingredients, use the best quality you can afford. If you're blending fruits into the mixture, make sure they are ripe. You can brighten the flavours in your ice pops with a squeeze of lemon or lime juice. A small pinch of salt also has the same effect.

TOOLS FOR THE JOB

To make ice lollies, the main bits of kitchen equipment you need are a large bowl, a spoon and some sort of mould to freeze them in. For plenty of recipes, this is all the equipment you will need, but there are a few extras that can help.

Blender
A good-quality blender is useful for puréeing fresh fruits with syrups and juices.

Juicer
A sturdy juicer will cut the time and mess in half when you're squeezing citrus fruits.

Saucepan
For making simple syrups and for simmering together mixes that benefit from a bit of heat infusion, like mulled wine or spice-infused milk.

Fine-mesh sieve
To strain mixtures. Especially useful if you want to make clear ice pops without the cloudiness that fruit pulps can create.

Kitchen scales, measuring cups and spoons
Digital scales can make measuring out ingredients easy – just put your mixing bowl on them and start pouring in the ingredients. Measuring cups and spoons are another option for weighing out ingredients. The ingredient weights in the book are given in grams, millilitres and spoons.

Jugs and ladles
Transferring the liquid mix into the moulds is easier if you use a jug with a spout or a small ladle.

Moulds and sticks

There are lots of ice-pop moulds on the market, and even some popsicle makers that will shape and set your ice lollies in under an hour. To test these recipes I used a mixture of soft silicone moulds and rigid plastic moulds, all around 65–100ml per ice pop.

As a rule of thumb, I found that fruit and syrup-based ice pops froze really well in the silicone moulds, while the dairy-based lollies tended to do better in a hard-sided plastic mould, especially if they had alcohol in them. If you do make a cream version in a soft mould and the mould is unwilling to let it go, even after you've dipped it in warm water, carefully insert a thin round-bladed knife and run it around the edge of the ice pop to loosen it. It should pull straight out.

You don't have to buy special moulds to make ice lollies, you can use freezer-proof shot glasses, tall, thin glasses, ice cube trays or disposable cups. Don't use anything too wide, though, like a tumbler or a bowl, as the ice pops can end up too thick, which slows down the freezing process and makes them too icy. Also remember that the stick has to be able to hold up the ice lolly – making a giant ice pop looks like fun until you unmould it and realise the only way you'll be able to eat it is from a bowl with a spoon and chisel.

Most moulds come either with stick holders (little slits cut into the mould lid that will hold the sticks snugly in place) or with plastic sticks set into individual lids. If you buy a mould that doesn't come with integral sticks, wooden sticks are the best option. They are cheap and your ice lollies will stick firmly onto them.

TRICKS & TECHNIQUES

Get ahead on the ice-pop-making process with these smart skills that will help you elevate your game.

Cooling your mix

When you're making ice lollies, you want the mixture to be at least at room temperature, if not colder, to make sure the freezing process doesn't take too long. If you're making ice pops with a simple syrup or with a heat-infused mixture and don't want to wait hours for it to cool down, you can speed up the process by using an ice bath. Fill your sink or a large bowl with plenty of ice, add a little cold water and set a wide bowl on top. Pour the hot liquid into the bowl and stir it for a few minutes. Leave the mixture for around 1 hour, stirring every 15 minutes, until it's cold and ready for freezing.

Filling your moulds

When you're adding your mixture to the mould, don't fill it right to the brim. You need to leave space for the ice lollies to expand as they freeze. Around 5mm should be sufficient.

Freezing your lollies

Set your freezer to its coldest setting and clear out a space on the bottom shelf so the moulds can sit upright. Freezing times vary, but I find that fruit juice and syrup-based ice pops take around 5–8 hours to set, while dairy or coconut milk-based lollies take 8–10 hours, and anything with alcohol in it is best left in the freezer for at least 12 hours to make sure it is solid.

If your moulds have integral sticks in the lids, you can put your ice pops straight into the freezer and leave them until morning. If you need to insert the sticks yourself, you normally need to let the ice lollies freeze a little first to thicken them up. Putting the sticks into the ice pops when they're liquid tends to result in the sticks freezing at crazy angles, making the lollies hard to eat. Sometimes ice pops made with dairy or coconut mixtures can be stiff enough to insert the sticks straight away, but for thinner mixtures, freeze them for around 2–3 hours until they're slushy – the amount of time will depend on how cold your freezer is and whether the lollies contain alcohol or not. When they're slushy, take the ice pops out of the freezer, insert the sticks and return the moulds to the deep freeze.

Layering your lollies

If you want to freeze different flavours in different layers, freeze the first layer in the mould for 2–3 hours until it's quite thick but still slushy. Don't freeze it until it's solid – you still need to be able to get the stick in. Once your first layer is thick, pour in the next layer, insert the stick and freeze again for the same amount of time, until thick. For a third or fourth layer, repeat the process (without adding extra sticks).

Adding stripes

If you're making an ice lolly with a thick, dairy-based mixture and a fruit purée, it can be fun to swirl them together to make stripes. Layer the two mixtures in your mould in alternate layers, then stir a knife or skewer through the mixture a couple of times to mingle them together. Insert the sticks and freeze.

Suspending ingredients

Adding chunks of chocolate or fruit to a liquid mixture normally results in the solid ingredients drifting to the bottom of the mould. The best way to make sure your choc chips and cherry chunks are evenly spread through the ice pop is to pour half the mixture into the mould, freeze for 2–3 hours until slushy, then gently drop in the ingredients, insert the sticks and freeze until set.

Unmoulding your lollies

Patient ice-pop makers can let their frozen treats sit in their moulds at room temperature for a couple of minutes, then easily pull them out. For a quicker unmoulding, fill a large bowl or sink with warm water (hand-hot is warm enough), then dip the moulds into the water for between 10 and 30 seconds. Check every so often to see if the ice pops are ready to come out. If the stick comes out by itself, the lollies have become too soft and need to go back into the freezer to re-set.

Storing your lollies

The best way to store your ice pops is in the moulds, but that's not always practical if your moulds are attached in one big block. If you're unmoulding a batch of ice pops in one go, but aren't eating them straight away, wrap them in greaseproof paper and store in ziplock freezer bags.

If the edges of the ice pops are a bit too soft when you unmould them, you can freeze them a second time to set the shape. Line a baking tray with greaseproof paper, lay the unmoulded ice pops on the tray and freeze for 30 minutes to 1 hour until solid. Don't leave them in the freezer overnight like this – they can start to develop freezer burn or pick up the flavours of other foods stored in the freezer. Once your ice pops are set, wrap them individually in greaseproof paper and pop them into ziplock freezer bags.

Ice lollies are best eaten within one week, but they will keep well enough in the freezer for up to a month.

THE SWEET STUFF

You can use all sorts of sweeteners in ice lollies – cane sugar in all its forms, maple syrup, honey, agave syrup, or even sweeteners like Xylitol or Stevia. A lot of the recipes in this book use simple syrup – a mixture of sugar and water boiled together to make a clear syrup. I like it because it's easy to make and easy to add to mixtures; it gives the ice pops a slightly softer, creamier texture; and you can add flavours to it to enhance the ice pops.

Simple syrup also keeps really well in the fridge, so it's worth making a big batch to keep you going for a few weeks. What you don't use in lollies, you could always add to cocktails (the straightforward drinking kind, rather than the frozen on a stick kind). The recipe opposite can easily be scaled up or down. The ratio is very easy: equal parts sugar and water.

SIMPLE SYRUP

MAKES 500ml

250g granulated sugar
250ml water

Tip the sugar into a saucepan and pour in the water. Set the pan on a medium-high heat and bring to the boil, without stirring. Once the liquid is boiling, set your timer for 2 minutes. After 2 minutes, take the pan off the heat and leave the syrup to cool. Transfer to a clean jar or tub, seal, and store in the fridge for up to 1 month.

ADDING FLAVOURS

You can add fresh herbs, dried spices or even citrus zest to the syrup to flavour it. Herbs that work well include rosemary, thyme, bay and mint. Just add 3–4 small sprigs to the sugar and water, then follow the recipe. When you transfer the syrup to a jar or tub, strain out the sprigs through a fine-mesh sieve. For a spiced syrup, try infusing a cinnamon stick, a few cardamom pods or a star anise with the syrup. For syrup with a bit of zing, add a few strips of lemon, lime or orange peel.

THE RECIPES

PALOMA
PALETAS

MAKES 10

The paloma is Mexico's favourite cocktail — even more popular
than the margarita. A mix of sweet and sour with a salty tang
from the tequila, it's a thirst-quenching and very moreish drink.
It makes an elegant ice lolly that I think is especially good as
a pre-dinner treat.

250ml Simple Syrup
(see page 19)
250ml fresh grapefruit juice
1 lime
60ml silver tequila
250ml fresh ruby
grapefruit juice

Make the simple syrup following the recipe on page
19, then leave it to cool.

Pour the regular grapefruit juice into a jug (keep the
ruby grapefruit juice for later). Squeeze in the juice
from half the lime (save the rest for later) and add
30ml of the tequila. Add 125ml of the simple syrup.
Stir to mix, pour the mixture into moulds and freeze
for 2–3 hours until slushy and semi-frozen.

Pour the remaining simple syrup and tequila into a
jug. Squeeze in the remaining lime juice. Stir in the
ruby grapefruit juice. Take the semi-frozen lollies out
of the freezer and pour in the ruby grapefruit mixture,
then insert sticks and freeze overnight until solid.

MANGO & YOGURT TWISTS

MAKES 6

Cheerful swirls of lime-spiked mango mingle with thick spoonfuls of just-sweet-enough Greek yogurt to make an ice lolly that would be perfect served as dessert after a dinner that is full of spice and chilli heat.

250g mango pulp or
   chopped fresh mango
4 tbsp icing sugar
Juice of ½ lime
450g Greek yogurt
1 tsp vanilla extract

If you're using chopped fresh mango, pop it into a small bowl and purée it with a hand-held blender or blitz in a blender until smooth. Add 2 tablespoons of the icing sugar and the lime juice to the pulp and either blitz again or use a spoon to beat it in. Put the yogurt into a separate bowl and add the remaining 2 tablespoons of icing sugar and the vanilla extract. Stir well to mix.

Spoon the yogurt and the mango pulp into your moulds in alternate layers until you've used them all up. Gently stir a butter knife through the yogurt and mango a few times to swirl them together. Insert sticks into the lollies and freeze overnight until solid.

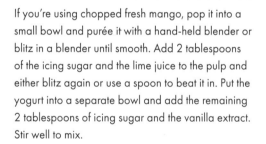

BLUEBERRY SKY POPS

MAKES 6–8

As up, up and away as any ice lolly can be. This recipe was inspired
by the Aviation – the turn-of-the-century cocktail invented to
celebrate the adventures of the first pilots taking to the skies in the
early 1900s. The cocktail gets its lilac-blue hue from crème de violette,
but for this lolly I thought a fruity hit of blueberry would be tastier.

100ml Simple Syrup
(see page 19)
400ml can coconut milk
125g blueberries
60ml London dry gin

Make the Simple Syrup following the recipe on
page 19, then let it cool.

Give the can of coconut milk a good shake to
make sure the coconut cream and water are mixed
together. Pour into a blender. Add the Simple Syrup
and blueberries. Blitz until combined and smooth.
You can add the gin and pulse again to combine, or
pour the mixture through a sieve into a jug to catch
any unblended pulp, then add the gin and stir.

Pour the mixture into moulds and freeze for 2–3
hours until slushy and semi-frozen. Insert sticks into
the lollies, then freeze overnight until set.

STRAWBERRY TEQUILA SUNRISE
ICE POPS

MAKES 10

These ice lollies have blushing red tops, thanks to a mix of grenadine and strawberries, and a cooling orange and tequila base. If you don't have grenadine, just use simple syrup instead (see the recipe on page 19) – the lollies will be pink rather than red, but just as tasty.

110g strawberries
100ml grenadine syrup
Juice of 1 lime
150ml Simple Syrup
  (see page 19)
450ml fresh orange juice
60ml silver tequila

Hull the strawberries then tip them into a blender. Add the grenadine syrup and half the lime juice. Blitz to make a smooth purée. Spoon the mixture into moulds and freeze for 2–3 hours until slushy and semi-frozen.

Make the Simple Syrup following the recipe on page 19, then let it cool.

Pour the remaining lime juice into a jug. Add the orange juice, Simple Syrup and the tequila and stir well. Pour the orange and tequila mixture into the moulds on top of the strawberry mix. Insert sticks into the lollies and freeze overnight until solid.

APRICOT & BAY PALETAS

MAKES 10

In Mexico, *paletas* are ice lollies typically made with fresh fruit, and the flavours change with the season. These glossy apricot ice lollies taste like early summer on a stick. When fresh apricots aren't available, you can use two 400g cans of apricots in fruit juice, drained, instead.

450g fresh apricots, halved and stoned
1 large bay leaf
150g caster sugar
150ml cold water
Juice of ½ lemon

Place the apricots in a saucepan and add the bay leaf, sugar and water. Set the pan on a medium heat, pop on a lid and bring to a gentle boil. When the liquid is just bubbling, turn the heat down a little and simmer for 5–10 minutes until the apricots break down and become soft and pulpy. Set aside to cool (see the tip on page 16 on using ice baths to cool your lolly mixes quickly).

When you're ready to make the *paletas*, pick out the bay leaf and discard it. Stir in the lemon juice. Use a hand-held blender to blitz the apricots into a smooth purée, or ladle everything into a blender and blitz. Pour the mixture into moulds and freeze for 2–3 hours until semi-frozen. Insert sticks and freeze overnight until solid.

CHERRY COLA
POPTAILS

MAKES 8–10

A tipsy, grown-up version of cherry cola with an extra
kick of bourbon that'll take you straight back to the 1980s
– shoulder pads and blue eye shadow optional.

650ml cola
Juice of 1 lime
30ml cherry liqueur
30ml bourbon

Pour the cola into a jug and let it sit for 1–2 hours
so it goes slightly flat.

Stir in the lime juice, cherry liqueur and bourbon.
Pour the mixture into moulds and freeze for
2–3 hours until semi-frozen. Insert sticks into
the slushy cola, then freeze overnight until solid.

GIN & TONIC
ICE LOLLIES

Whether you like juniper-heavy London dry gins, malty Old Toms or botanical-rich artisanal gins, these lollies are a must for G&T fans. The tonic water and citrus give them a crisp, zingy edge. Just add your favourite gin.

650ml tonic water
100ml Simple Syrup
(see page 19)
½ lemon, ½ lime and a
chunk of cucumber
30ml fresh lime or lemon
juice
60ml good-quality gin

Pour the tonic water into a jug and leave it for 1–2 hours to go slightly flat.

Make the Simple Syrup following the recipe on page 19, then let it cool.

Thinly slice the lemon and lime halves and a small chunk of cucumber, then add a few slices of each to the moulds. Stir the Simple Syrup, lime or lemon juice and gin into the tonic water.

Pour the mixture into moulds and freeze for 2–3 hours until slushy and semi-frozen. Insert sticks and freeze overnight until solid.

BERRY BREAKFAST YOGURT POPS

MAKES 10

The ingredients in these yogurt pops – Greek yogurt, milk, honey, berries and granola – are no different from your regular breakfast bowl. They're just a lot more fun to eat when they're served on a stick.

110g mixed berries, such as strawberries, blueberries and raspberries
300g Greek yogurt
200ml whole milk
75g honey
75g granola

If you're using strawberries, hull them and then thinly slice or roughly chop them. Spoon the Greek yogurt into a mixing bowl, then add the milk and honey. Whisk together until smooth and combined. Stir in the berries.

Spoon the mixture into the moulds, leaving a small gap at the top of each mould, around 2cm. Sprinkle over the granola evenly over each mould. Insert a stick into each mould and freeze overnight until solid.

PEPPERMINT MARTINI
ICE POPS

MAKES 8–10

One way to make wrapping presents for Christmas more fun is to mix yourself a candy cane martini – a peppermint twist on a vodka martini – to sip while you stick and snip ribbons and paper. Inspired by that festive treat, I mixed up a batch of these mint-and-coconut lollies that have a snowy texture and a wintry flavour.

397g can sweetened
   condensed milk
250ml coconut milk
25g coconut cream
60ml good-quality vodka
1 tsp peppermint extract

Pour the condensed milk and coconut milk into a mixing bowl and whisk together until smooth. Crumble in the coconut cream and whisk to combine. Add the vodka and peppermint extract and whisk again briefly.

Use a small ladle to pour the mixture into moulds, or transfer the mix to a jug and pour in. Freeze for 2–3 hours, then insert sticks and freeze overnight until solid.

SEA BREEZER
POPS

In the 1990s, no bar menu was complete unless it had a Sea Breeze on it. A dry mix of cranberry, grapefruit, lime and vodka, it was the drink of the summer – every summer – until the Cosmopolitan came along to claim its crown. Turned into a tangy frozen poptail, the Sea Breeze can hold its head up high once again.

. . . .

200ml Simple Syrup (see page 19)
250ml ruby grapefruit juice
250ml cranberry juice
Juice of 2 limes
60ml good-quality vodka

. . . .

Make the Simple Syrup following the recipe on page 19, then let it cool.

Pour the grapefruit juice into a jug and add the cranberry juice, fresh lime juice and vodka. Add the cooled Simple Syrup and stir to mix everything together.

Pour the mixture into moulds and freeze for 2–3 hours until slushy and semi-frozen. Insert sticks and freeze overnight until solid.

STRAWBERRY SIDECAR FREEZIES

MAKES 8–10

Put some Parisian chic into your ice lollies by basing them on the Sidecar, a brandy cocktail invented in a Paris bistro and named after the motorcycle sidecar that brought a favourite customer to and from the bar.

350ml Simple Syrup
(see page 19)
110g strawberries
200ml fresh lemon juice
100ml cold water
30ml brandy
30ml triple sec

Make the Simple Syrup following the recipe on page 19, then let it cool.

Hull the strawberries and pop them in a blender. Add the Simple Syrup, lemon juice and water and blitz until smooth. You can add the brandy and triple sec and pulse again to combine; or pour the mixture through a sieve into a jug to catch any unblended pulp, then add the brandy and triple sec and stir.

Pour the mixture into mould and freeze for 2–3 hours until semi-frozen. Insert sticks into the slushy lollies and freeze for another 5–6 hours until solid.

STRAWBERRY & BOURBON TWISTS

MAKES 10–12

A single-serve strawberry ice cream that takes five minutes to make and comes with a bonus hit of bourbon for vanilla richness.

110g strawberries
1 tbsp. lemon juice
397g can sweetened condensed milk
250ml double cream
250ml whole milk
60ml bourbon

Hull the strawberries then tip them into a bowl. Add the lemon juice and use a hand-held blender to blitz into a purée. No blender? Use a fork to crush the strawberries and stir in the lemon juice. Set aside.

Pour the condensed milk and double cream into a mixing bowl and whisk together until smooth. Whisk in the milk. Add the strawberry purée and bourbon and gently stir to just combine.

Use a small ladle to pour the mixture into moulds, or transfer the mix to a jug and pour it in. Insert the sticks, then freeze overnight until solid.

BLOOD ORANGE
FROGRONIS

MAKES 8–10

A Frogroni is a Negroni that's spent a few hours in the deep freeze. Blood oranges are a new year treat and the juice is brilliant blended with the mix of gin, Campari and sweet vermouth to make a fruity version of the famous Italian aperitivo. Be careful when you're measuring out the spirits — more than 60ml in the mix will stop the lollies from freezing.

250ml Simple Syrup
   (see page 19)
450ml fresh blood orange
   juice
20ml Campari
20ml London dry gin
20ml sweet red vermouth

Make the Simple Syrup following the recipe on page 19, then let it cool.

When you're ready to make the lollies, pour the Simple Syrup into a jug. Add the blood orange juice, Campari, gin and vermouth. Stir well. For clear lollies, pour the mix through a sieve to catch any orange pulp. Don't press the pulp to squeeze out any remaining juice — that will make the ice pops cloudy.

Pour the mixture into moulds and freeze for about 2–3 hours until slushy and semi-frozen. Insert sticks into the lollies, then freeze overnight until solid.

BELLINI
ICE POPS

MAKES 10

Sitting on the terrace of Harry's Bar in Venice and sipping a fresh peach Bellini has always been on my bucket list. I haven't made it there just yet, but in the meantime these fizzy peach ice pops are the next best thing. When you're picking a prosecco, go for one labelled 'brut', which is dry but still fresh and fruity.

· ·

100ml Simple Syrup (see page 19)
200ml brut prosecco
400g can peaches in fruit juice

· ·

Make the Simple Syrup following the recipe on page 19, then leave it to cool.

Pour the prosecco into a jug or bowl and leave it for 1 hour to go slightly flat.

When you're ready to make the lollies, tip the canned peaches and their juice into a blender, add the Simple Syrup and blitz to combine. Pour in the prosecco and blitz again briefly. Pour the mixture into moulds and freeze for 2–3 hours until semi-frozen. Insert sticks and freeze overnight until set.

CUBA LIBRE
LOLLIES

MAKES 8–10

This icy version of the classic Cuban cocktail is one delicious way to stay cool when the nights are as hot as they are in Havana. Cola is great frozen. The sweetness becomes refreshing, and adding a sharp dash of lime brings out the aromatic spices. Adding the rum just makes the lollies fun.

650ml cola
½ lemon
½ lime
60ml white rum
Juice of 1 lime
A few dashes of Angostura bitters

Pour the cola into a jug and let it sit for 1–2 hours to go slightly flat.

Finely slice the lemon and lime halves, then drop a slice of each into each lolly mould.

Add the white rum and lime juice to the cola with a few dashes of Angostura bitters (4–5 good shakes should do it). Stir together, then pour into the moulds and freeze for 2–3 hours until slushy and semi-frozen. Insert the sticks and freeze overnight until solid.

AVOCADO & COCONUT ICE STICKS

MAKES 8

Buttery avocados are amazing in ice lollies. They have a luxurious texture that's just as good as cream or yogurt for creating a rich, luscious consistency. These avocado and coconut ice sticks are balanced between sweet and savoury, so they feel indulgent and a bit good for you, too.

2 ripe avocados (weighing around 400g, including skin and stones)
250ml coconut milk
2 tbsp. maple or agave syrup
Juice of ½ lime
A pinch of flaky sea salt
3–4 tbsp. cold water (optional)
60ml white or coconut rum

Halve the avocados, scoop out the stones and then scoop the flesh into a blender. If the coconut milk is in a can, give it a really good shake to mix the coconut cream and water together, then measure out 250ml and add it to the blender. Add the maple or agave syrup, lime juice, rum and a pinch of sea salt. Blitz until smooth and combined. If the mixture seems a bit thick, add some or all of the water and blitz again. Spoon the mixture into moulds, insert the sticks and freeze overnight until firm.

MOSCOW MULE
ICE POPS

MAKES 10

The Moscow Mule was supposed to have been invented
in the Cock 'n' Bull Saloon on Sunset Strip in the 1940s. It was
called 'the cocktail with a kick', and these fiery ice pops, packed
with ginger heat and vodka, will definitely get your taste
buds buzzing.

650ml ginger beer
60ml good-quality vodka
Juice of 2 limes

Pour the ginger beer into a jug and let it sit on the
side for 1–2 hours so it goes slightly flat.

When you're ready to make the ice pops, add the
vodka and lime juice to the ginger beer. Stir well,
then pour the mixture into moulds and freeze for
2–3 hours until slushy and semi-frozen. Insert the
sticks, then freeze overnight until solid.

ORANGE & APEROL SPRITZICLES

Sometime in the early 2000s Aperol Spritzes escaped from the Venetian bars where they're a pre-dinner essential and started to take over the world. Now no self-respecting bar opens up without a spritz on the menu. The original drink is always made with Aperol, but other bitter Italian aperitifs like Campari and Cynar work just as well, and you can swap them into this ice lolly recipe, too.

200ml Simple Syrup
   (see page 19)
200ml brut prosecco
250ml fresh orange juice
60ml Aperol

Make the Simple Syrup following the recipe on page 19, then leave it to cool.

Pour the prosecco into a jug or bowl and let it sit for 1 hour to go slightly flat.

When you're ready to make the lollies, add the Simple Syrup to the prosecco and pour in the orange juice and Aperol. Stir to mix. Pour the mixture into moulds and freeze for 2–3 hours until semi-frozen. Insert sticks into the moulds and freeze overnight until set.

ICE ICE BAILEYS

MAKES 8

When I told friends I was writing a book of boozy ice lollies, they all said the same thing: 'Make one with Baileys!' So I can guarantee that all your friends will want to try these ice lollies, too. There are two ways to make them: without cocoa, which gives you a straight-up, creamy Baileys-flavoured ice lolly; or with cocoa, which turns the mix into an outrageously decadent frozen chocolate mousse.

500ml whole milk
100g caster sugar
2 tbsp. unsweetened cocoa powder (optional)
100ml Baileys Original Irish Cream
Chocolate sprinkles, to serve

Pour the milk into a saucepan and add the sugar and cocoa powder, if you're using it. Whisk together until combined, then place the pan on a medium heat and bring to a gentle boil – keep your eye on it, don't let it boil over. When the milk is just boiling, turn the heat down a little and simmer for 2 minutes, stirring. Pour the hot milk into a heatproof jug and set aside for 1–2 hours to cool (see the tip on page 16 on using ice baths to cool your mixture quickly).

Stir the Baileys into the cooled milk. Pour the mixture into moulds and freeze for 2–3 hours until thickened and semi-frozen. Insert the sticks, then freeze overnight until solid.

To serve, unmould and scatter over a few chocolate sprinkles.

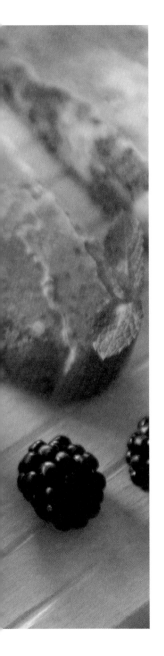

ICED
BRAMBLES

MAKES 10

The Bramble was invented in the 1980s by legendary London bartender Dick Bradsell. He was inspired by his boyhood summers spent in the countryside, picking blackberries and getting scratched by brambles. If you've been blackberrying and have more fruits than you can bake into a pie, turn a few into these simple, nostalgic ice lollies.

· ·

110g blackberries
50g icing sugar
650ml whole milk
Juice of ½ lime
60ml London dry gin

· ·

Tip the blackberries into your blender. Add the icing sugar and pour in the milk and lime juice. Blitz until smooth and combined. Pour in the gin and pulse briefly to mix it in.

Pour the mixture into moulds and freeze for 2–3 hours until semi-frozen. Insert sticks into the moulds and freeze overnight until solid.

RUM & COCONUT COOLERS

MAKES 6

These creamy coconut ice pops come with a dash of lime and a slosh of white rum. They're easy to make and a quicker way to take yourself to the Caribbean than getting on a plane.

100ml Simple Syrup (see page 19)
400ml can coconut milk
60ml white rum
Juice of 1 lime
A few pinches of dessicated coconut

Make the Simple Syrup following the recipe on page 19, then leave it to cool.

Give the can of coconut milk a good shake to make sure the coconut cream and water are mixed together. Pour into a jug. Add the Simple Syrup, white rum and lime juice and stir well.

Pour the coconut mixture into moulds and freeze for 2–3 hours until slushy and semi-frozen. Sprinkle a few pinches of desiccated coconut into the moulds, insert sticks, then freeze overnight until set.

CHOCOLATE CHERRY RIPPLES

MAKES 8–10

A lolly of two halves, both featuring juicy fresh cherries.
The bottom layer is a classic mix of Greek yogurt and honey,
while the top has a bittersweet swirl of cocoa powder
stirred through it.

● ● ● ● ● ● ● ● ● ● ● ● ● ● ●

300g Greek yogurt
300ml whole milk
4 tbsp. honey
1 heaped tbsp unsweetened
   cocoa powder
75g fresh cherries, halved
   and stoned

● ●

Spoon half the Greek yogurt into a mixing bowl,
then add half the milk and half the honey and whisk
together. Tip in the cocoa powder and use a spatula
to fold everything together. Ladle the chocolate
mixture into the lolly moulds, filling them so they
are half- to three-quarters full. Drop in a few cherry
halves. Slide the moulds into the freezer and freeze
for 2 hours.

When the lollies are just starting to set, whisk the
remaining yogurt, milk and honey together in
a bowl. Spoon it into the moulds, drop in a few
more cherry halves, insert the sticks and freeze for
another 5–6 hours or overnight until solid.

EASY WATERMELON

FREEZER POPS

MAKES 8–10

This recipe is so simple it isn't really a recipe at all. But when summer is here, hot and blazing, you'll be glad you have a stack of these watermelon wedges in your freezer. They take a few minutes to assemble and, eaten straight from the freezer, they have a crunchy, almost granita-like texture. If you don't mind sticky fingers, squeeze a little lime juice over them just before eating. It brings out the melon's sweetness.

A wedge of watermelon
1 lime
Vodka, to serve

Line a baking tray with baking paper. Slice the watermelon into triangle-shaped pieces around 2–3cm thick. Insert a small, sharp knife into the rind in the middle of each wedge to create a little opening. Insert a stick into each opening, then place the watermelon slices on the tray. Slide into the freezer and freeze overnight.

Wrap the watermelon pops in baking paper and store them in a freezerproof tub. These pops are best eaten within one week of making.

Pour a large measure of ice-cold vodka into tumblers and place a watermelon pop in each glass to serve

PINK LEMONADE
ICE LOLLIES

MAKES 8–10

Take a trip back to your childhood with these nostalgic ice lollies.
They get their pale pink colour from a handful of strawberries blitzed
with simple syrup and fresh lemon juice. The mixture will taste very
sweet when you make it, but once it's frozen the sugar balances out
with the sharp lemon juice to make a really refreshing treat.

350ml Simple Syrup
(see page 19)
110g strawberries
200ml fresh lemon juice
150ml cold water
60ml vodka

Make the Simple Syrup following the recipe on
page 19, then let it cool.

Hull the strawberries and pop them in a blender.
Add the Simple Syrup, lemon juice, vodka and
water and blitz until smooth. If you'd like clear
lollies, pour the mixture through a sieve to catch
any unblended seeds or pulp. Don't press the pulp
to squeeze out any remaining juice – that will make
the lollies cloudy.

Pour the mixture into moulds and freeze for 2–3
hours until semi-frozen. Insert the sticks into the
slushy lollies and freeze for another 3–5 hours
until solid.

CHERRY KIRSCH
KICKS

MAKES 10

Every June in Zug, in Northern Switzerland, the
Chriesigloggä (cherry bell) rings out, marking the start of the cherry
harvest. Cherries are a big deal in Zug, where the season is celebrated
with a 300-year-old race through the old town, and a special market
that sells fresh cherries and cherry products. You can try fresh cherries
and cherry products, including a liqueur called kirschwasser. It is drier
than other cherry liqueurs, so serving kirschwasser with a small lemon
ice lolly makes it refreshing rather than sweet.

350ml Simple Syrup
   (see page 19)
200ml fresh lemon juice
150ml cold water
75g fresh cherries, halved
   and stoned
350ml chilled kirschwasser
   or cherry liqueur

Make the Simple Syrup following the recipe on
page 19, then leave it to cool.

Pour the Simple Syrup, lemon juice and water into
a jug and stir to combine. Pour the mixture into
moulds. Freeze for 2–3 hours until just starting to
freeze, then gently press the halved cherries into the
slushy lollies and insert the sticks. Freeze for another
6–8 hours until solid.

To serve, pour a large measure of kirschwasser
into each glass, unmould the lollies and serve them
dunked in the kirschwasser.

RASPBERRY RUSSIAN

RIPPLES

MAKES 8–10

In *The Big Lebowski*, the Dude drinks nine White Russians – a sticky drink made with vodka, coffee liqueur and cream that was buried at the bottom of bar menus until the Coen brothers gave it a supporting role in their movie. To turn it into a frozen version, I added raspberries to lighten up the dairy, along with a dash of crème de cacao for a rich hint of chocolate.

75ml Simple Syrup
  (see page 19)
110g raspberries
300ml double cream
200ml whole milk
30ml good-quality vodka
30ml crème de cacao
  white liqueur

Make the Simple Syrup following the recipe on page 19, then let it cool.

Tip the raspberries into a small bowl and roughly crush them with a fork. Set aside. Pour the cream into a mixing bowl and whisk until it starts to thicken slightly. Pour in the milk, Simple Syrup, vodka and crème de cacao. Whisk together until smooth and combined. Gently fold in the crushed berries to just mix. Spoon the mixture into the moulds, insert a stick into each mould and freeze overnight until solid.

STRAWBERRY FROSÉ
ICE POPS

MAKES 10

A frosé is a frozen rosé that's normally served as a slushy.
Keep it in the freezer overnight and you get fruity ice pops,
like these.

100ml Simple Syrup
(see page 19)
250g strawberries
350ml dry rosé wine
150ml ruby grapefruit juice
Juice of 2 limes
A pinch of flaky sea salt

Make the Simple Syrup following the recipe on page 19, then let it cool.

Hull the strawberries and tip them into a blender. Pour in the rosé wine, ruby grapefruit juice, lime juice and Simple Syrup. Add a small pinch of sea salt. Blitz until smooth and combined. Pour through a sieve into a jug, and use the back of a spoon to press any pulp that collects in the sieve to squeeze out any remaining juice.

Pour the mixture into moulds and freeze for 2–3 hours until slushy and semi-frozen. Insert sticks and freeze overnight until solid.

LIME & GIN GIMLET POPTAILS

MAKES 10

A 50:50 mix of gin and lime cordial, the Gimlet is a cocktail that made its way around the world with the English navy, whose sailors drank it for its 'medicinal' benefits. Turned into an ice lolly, it's sweet and sharp with a botanical twist, thanks to the gin.

350ml Simple Syrup
  (see page 19)
200ml fresh lime juice
150ml cold water
60ml London dry gin
1 lime, to serve

Make the Simple Syrup following the recipe on page 19, then leave it to cool.

When you're ready to make the lollies, pour the Simple Syrup, lime juice, water and gin into a jug and stir to mix.

Pour the mixture into moulds. Freeze for 2–3 hours until semi-frozen. Slice the lime and push a slice into each semi-frozen lolly, then insert the sticks and freeze overnight until solid.

STRAWBERRIES & CREAM
ICE POPS

MAKES 12

Like a boozy strawberry milkshake that's taken a trip to Siberia, these quick, creamy ice pops have a fluffy texture and a moreish berry sweetness.

100ml Simple Syrup
  (see page 19)
110g strawberries
397g can sweetened
  condensed milk
250ml double cream
250ml whole milk
1 tsp vanilla extract
60ml good-quality vodka

Make the Simple Syrup following the recipe on page 19, then let it cool.

Hull and chop the strawberries. Tip them into your blender, add the Simple Syrup and blitz until you have a smooth purée. Scoop the condensed milk into the blender, then pour in the cream, milk, vanilla extract and vodka. Pulse a few times to lightly mix everything together. Pour the mixture into moulds and freeze for 2–3 hours until semi-frozen. Insert sticks into the moulds and freeze overnight until set.

MINTED BOURBON & LIME LOLLIES

MAKES 10

A Kentucky classic, a Mint Julep is an excellent way to cool down on hot and humid summer days. This frozen take on the super-chilled bourbon cocktail is based around lime juice, which gives these ice pops a mouthwatering sharpness sweetened by a mint-spiked sugar syrup.

350ml mint-infused Simple Syrup (see page 19)
200ml fresh lime juice
150ml cold water
60ml bourbon
A few drops of green food colouring, optional

Make the Simple Syrup following the recipe on page 19, then let it cool.

When you want to make the lollies, pour the Simple Syrup, lime juice, water and bourbon into a jug and stir to mix. If you are using green food colouring, add a few drops to the mix and stir.

Pour the mixture into moulds and freeze for 3 hours until semi-frozen. Insert the sticks into the slushy lollies and freeze for 6–8 hours until solid.

SCREWDRIVER
ICE POPS

MAKES 8

How do you mix a cocktail when you're out in the oil fields of the Persian Gulf and you forgot to pack your bar spoon? Use a screwdriver, of course. That's what American oil workers did back in the mid-twentieth century, and it's how the Screwdriver got its name. At least, that's how one story goes. However it got its name, it's a great drink that's perfect for turning into a poptail.

200ml Simple Syrup
  (see page 19)
½ orange
450ml fresh orange juice
60ml good-quality vodka
A few dashes of Angostura
  bitters

Make the Simple Syrup following the recipe on page 19, then leave it to cool.

Slice the orange half into 8 thin slices. Pop 1 slice into each mould. Pour the orange juice into a jug and add the Simple Syrup, vodka and a few dashes of Angostura bitters (4–5 good shakes should do it). Stir to mix.

Pour the orange mixture into the moulds and freeze for 2–3 hours, until semi-frozen. Insert the sticks into the slushy lollies and freeze for 3–5 hours until solid.

DRUNKEN MONKEY
POPTAILS

Naughty monkeys who like a stiff drink will enjoy these liqueur-spiked ice lollies that mix the velvety richness of coconut milk with a dark hit of cocoa. Crème de banane is a bit niche, but its sugary, tropical flavour suits this recipe perfectly. If you'd like to swap it for something else, try coconut rum, crème de cacao or brandy.

● ●

100ml maple syrup
400ml can coconut milk
2 tbsp unsweetened cocoa powder
60ml crème de banane
A pinch of flaky sea salt
1 small banana

Pour the maple syrup into a bowl. Give the can of coconut milk a really good shake to mix the coconut cream and water together, then pour it into the maple syrup. Add the cocoa powder and gently whisk until combined. Add the crème de banane and a pinch of sea salt and stir to combine.

Peel and chop the banana into 20 slices. Drop the banana slices evenly among the lolly moulds, then pour in the coconut mixture and freeze for 2 hours until semi-frozen. Insert sticks into the lollies and freeze until solid.

SEX ON THE BEACH
ICE STICKS

MAKES 10

Fun, fruity and just a little flirty, Sex on the Beach is the essential holiday cocktail. The mix of sweet fruit juices with a kick of booze from schnapps and vodka works brilliantly in an ice lolly, too.

200ml Simple Syrup (see page 19)
200ml pineapple juice
200ml cranberry juice
200ml fresh orange juice
30ml peach schnapps
30ml good-quality vodka

Make the Simple Syrup following the recipe on page 19, then let it cool.

Pour the pineapple juice into a jug and add the cranberry juice, orange juice, peach schnapps and vodka. Pour in the cooled Simple Syrup and stir to mix everything together.

Pour the mixture into moulds and freeze for 2–3 hours until slushy and semi-frozen. Insert sticks and freeze overnight until solid.

IRISH COFFEE PUDDING POPS

MAKES 10

An Irish coffee after dinner is a treat on cold, wet evenings, but in the summer I want something more refreshing, which is where these indulgent ice lollies come in. The Demerara sugar adds a touch of toffee to the mix of bitter coffee and malted whiskey.

200ml hot filter coffee
100g Demerara sugar
400ml single cream
60ml Irish whiskey
75g chocolate chips

Pour the coffee into a heatproof jug, add the Demerara sugar and stir until the sugar has dissolved. Set aside to cool (see the tip on page 16 on using ice baths to cool your lolly mixes quickly).

When the coffee is cool, stir in the cream and Irish whiskey. Pour the Irish coffee mixture into moulds and freeze for 2 hours until semi-frozen. Sprinkle the chocolate chips into the moulds and stir gently with a butter knife or skewer to mix them in. Insert sticks into the lollies and freeze overnight until solid.

PERSIMMON & BOURBON
ICE SHOTS

These fruity lollies are sorbet on a stick. Made with honey-fleshed persimmons blitzed with a little sugar and fresh citrus, they have a velvety texture and a sweet sherbet flavour that is delicious paired with an oak-soaked, cask-aged bourbon.

300g ripe persimmons, chopped
2 heaped tbsp. caster sugar
150ml fresh clementine juice
60ml bourbon
Juice of ½ lime

Tip the chopped persimmons into a blender and add the sugar, clementine juice, bourbon and lime juice. Blitz until blended and smooth.

Pour the mixture into moulds (don't be tempted to sieve it – the pulp gives the lollies their soft, silky texture) – then insert sticks and freeze overnight until solid.

COLD FASHIONEDS

Did Don Draper ever stop for an ice pop in *Mad Men*? If he didn't, it's probably because no one thought to turn his favourite cocktail – the Old Fashioned – into a frozen treat. This orange-juice-based version keeps the bourbon up front, which adds a dash of brown-sugar sweetness to the intense, crisp citrus.

200ml Simple Syrup (see page 19)
450ml fresh orange juice
60ml bourbon
A few dashes of Angostura bitters

Make the Simple Syrup following the recipe on page 19, then leave it to cool.

Pour the orange juice into a jug and add the Simple Syrup, bourbon and a few dashes of Angostura bitters (4–5 good shakes should do it). Stir to mix, then pour the orange mixture into the moulds. Freeze for 2–3 hours, until semi-frozen. Insert the sticks into the slushy lollies and freeze for 3–5 hours until solid.

BLUEBERRY CHEESECAKE POPS

MAKES 6

The mix of Greek yogurt and cream cheese in these cheesecake pops gives them a tart and tangy flavour that's sweetened by a little honey. I've left it up to you how much honey you add; go for less if you want the sharpness of the blueberries to shine through, or add more for a richer, more luscious flavour. Whatever you do, don't skip the salt. It adds a savoury note that, in a slice of cheesecake, would come from the biscuit crust.

75g blueberries
225g Greek yogurt
225g full-fat cream cheese
2–4 tbsp. honey
Juice of ½ lime
A pinch of flaky sea salt

Roughly chop the blueberries. Spoon the Greek yogurt and cream cheese into a mixing bowl. Add the honey (use 2 tablespoons for a tart flavour, 4 tablespoons for something sweeter), the lime juice and a pinch of sea salt. Whisk together until smooth and combined. Add the chopped blueberries and use a spoon to fold them into the mixture. Use a small spoon to divide the mixture between moulds. Insert the sticks and freeze overnight.

CUCUMBER MARTINI COOLERS

MAKES 10

The nearest thing to the taste of an English country garden in lolly form. The green cucumber flavour is front and centre, but if you'd like something a little more aromatic, swap the vodka for your favourite gin.

100ml Simple Syrup (see page 19)
600g roughly chopped cucumber
Juice of ½ lime
60ml good-quality vodka

Make the Simple Syrup following the recipe on page 19, then let it cool.

Tip the cucumber into a blender. Add the Simple Syrup, lime juice and vodka. Blitz until blended and smooth. For smooth lollies, pour the mixture through a sieve into a jug to catch any unblended pulp. Press the pulp to squeeze out as much juice as possible. Pour the mixture into moulds and freeze for 2–3 hours until semi-frozen. Insert sticks into the moulds and freeze overnight until set.

STRAWBERRY & PEACH DAIQUIRI POPS

A triple-decker take on the classic Caribbean cocktail
that sandwiches a cool and creamy coconut layer between
two fruity Daiquiri twists: peach on the bottom, strawberry on the top.
The chia seeds add texture to the lollies, but you can leave
them out if you prefer.

For the strawberry layer:
100ml Simple Syrup
  (see page 19)
150g strawberries
Juice of ½ lime
30ml white rum

For the coconut layer:
200ml coconut milk
10g chia seeds

For the peach layer:
250g fresh peaches,
  stoned and chopped
2 tbsp icing sugar
30ml white rum

Make the Simple Syrup following the recipe on page 19, then let it cool.

Hull and chop the strawberries, then tip into a blender and add the Simple Syrup, lime juice and white rum. Blitz until smooth and combined. Ladle the strawberry purée into the moulds, or transfer to a jug and pour it in. Freeze for 2–3 hours until semi-frozen.

About 40 minutes before you want to add the second layer. Pour the coconut milk into a bowl and whisk to make sure it is smooth and combined. Add the chia seeds and stir to mix. Set aside for 30 minutes to let the chia seeds expand. Take the moulds out of the freezer and layer the coconut and chia seed mix into the moulds. Insert the lolly sticks and return to the freezer for another 3 hours.

Make the final layer by tipping the chopped peaches into a blender with the icing sugar and white rum. Pulse to make a smooth purée. Take the moulds out of the freezer and ladle the mixture into them. Return to the freezer for another 4–5 hours until solid.

CARIBBEAN COCONUT

ICE STICKS

MAKES 10

On the island of Jost Van Dyke, in the Caribbean, there is a beach bar called the Soggy Dollar. Most of its customers are sailors, but there's no dock so they have to swim ashore and pay for their drinks with wet dollar bills. Apart from being full of waterlogged drinkers, the Soggy Dollar is famous for inventing the Painkiller – a rum and coconut tiki drink that tastes like summer by the sea. This frozen version is based around coconut milk with a dash of dark rum.

100ml Simple Syrup
   (see page 19)
400ml can coconut milk
75ml pineapple juice
75ml fresh orange juice
60ml dark rum

Make the Simple Syrup following the recipe on page 19, then let it cool.

Give the can of coconut milk a good shake to make sure the coconut cream and water are mixed together. Pour into a jug. Add the Simple Syrup, pineapple juice, orange juice and dark rum and stir well.

Pour the coconut mixture into moulds and freeze for 2–3 hours until slushy and semi-frozen. Insert sticks into the lollies, and freeze overnight until solid.

GRAPEFRUIT & BOURBON
POPTAILS

MAKES 8

The Brown Derby is a cocktail straight out of the 1920s. A simple sour, it's the kind of mixed drink that's easy to turn into an ice lolly because the same three elements that make it a great cocktail (sweetness, sourness and boozy heat) also make it perfect as an ice lolly.

• •

200ml rosemary-infused Simple Syrup
   (see page 19)
450ml fresh grapefruit juice
60ml bourbon

• •

Make the Simple Syrup following the recipe on page 19, then let it cool.

Pour the grapefruit juice into a jug and add the Simple Syrup, straining out the rosemary sprigs, and the bourbon. Stir to mix, then pour the mixture into the moulds. Freeze for 2–3 hours, until semi-frozen. Insert the sticks into the slushy lollies and freeze for 6–8 hours until solid.

103

DO-IT-YOURSELF
CHOC ICES

MAKES 10

The kind of DIY I'm happy to get involved in, these luxurious lollies
are made from a quick, no-churn ice cream and served with a warm,
boozy chocolate sauce that you can dunk your choc ice into or drizzle
over. I like dunking, because the lollies melt into the sauce, turning it
into a lush chocolate pudding.

For the ice cream bars:
397g can sweetened
   condensed milk
250ml double cream
250ml whole milk
1 tsp. vanilla extract
A pinch of flaky sea salt

For the chocolate sauce:
200g dark chocolate
100ml double cream
25g unsalted butter
2 tbsp. maple syrup
60ml brandy or dark rum
A pinch of flaky sea salt

To make the ice cream bars, pour the condensed
milk and double cream into a mixing bowl and
whisk together until combined and smooth. Whisk
in the milk. Add the vanilla extract and a pinch of
salt and whisk again briefly to combine. Use a small
ladle to pour the mixture into moulds, or transfer the
mix to a jug and pour. Freeze for 2–3 hours, then
insert the sticks and freeze overnight.

Make the chocolate sauce by chopping the chocolate
into small chunks and putting them in a heatproof
bowl. Set aside. Pour the cream into a saucepan and
add the butter and maple syrup. Set on a low heat
gently warm until steaming. Pour over the chocolate
and stir until the chocolate has melted and everything
is smoothly combined. Add the brandy or rum and a
pinch of salt and stir together. Ladle the warm sauce
into small bowls and serve with the ice cream bars.
Dip the bars in the sauce or spoon it over them and –
very messily – eat.

CANTALOUPE COOLERS

MAKES 10

Cantaloupe melons are floral and musky, with a mellow sweetness that pairs beautifully with the sunny smoothness of silver tequila. Add a layer of vanilla-scented Greek yogurt and you've got an ice pop worth lingering over.

100ml Simple Syrup (see page 19)
150g cantaloupe melon, chopped
100ml fresh orange juice
60ml silver tequila
450g Greek yogurt
2 tbsp. icing sugar
1 tsp. vanilla extract

Make the Simple Syrup following the recipe on page 19, then let it cool.

Tip the melon into a blender and add the Simple Syrup, orange juice and tequila. Blitz until smooth and combined. Pour the melon purée into moulds and freeze for 2–3 hours until semi-frozen.

Spoon the yogurt into a bowl and add the icing sugar and vanilla extract. Stir well to mix.
Take the moulds out of the freezer, spoon in the yogurt mixture, then insert the sticks and freeze overnight until solid.

ESPRESSO MARTINI
ICE POPS

MAKES 6–8

A brunch favourite, Espresso Martinis have the magic effect of waking you up and making you mellow at the same time. These lollies don't pack quite the same punch, but they would make a great sweet treat after stacks of pancakes on a Sunday morning.

30ml espresso
500ml whole milk
125g caster sugar
1 tsp. vanilla extract
60ml good-quality vodka

Pour the espresso and milk into a pan. Add the sugar and set the pan on a medium heat. Gently warm, stirring often, until the pan is steaming and just starting to boil. Turn the heat down and keep it on a gentle simmer for a few minutes, stirring often, until the sugar has dissolved. Set aside to cool (see the tip on page 16 on how to use an ice bath to cool your mixture quickly).

When you're ready to make the lollies, whisk in the vanilla extract and vodka, then pour the mixture into moulds. Freeze for 2–3 hours until semi-frozen. Insert sticks into the moulds and freeze overnight until set.

PASSION FRUIT & VODKA RIPPLES

MAKES 4–6

The inspiration for these indulgent ice pops is the Pornstar Martini, the flamboyant vodka cocktail that comes with a dash of vanilla, half a passion fruit and a shot of prosecco on the side. Combined with tangy Greek yogurt, the trio of vodka, vanilla and passion fruit make a not-too-sweet summer treat. Prosecco optional.

Pulp of 3 passion fruits, around 75g
4 tbsp icing sugar
60ml good-quality vodka
450g Greek yogurt
1 tsp. vanilla extract

Scoop the passion fruit pulp into a bowl, add the icing sugar and the vodka and gently stir to mix them together and dissolve the icing sugar. Add the Greek yogurt and vanilla extract and stir a few times to just mix everything together. Spoon the mixture into lolly moulds, insert the sticks and freeze overnight until solid.

PEACH SANGRIA
ICE POPS

These pretty ice pops are made with a lighter version of Spanish sangria, using rosé wine and adding a hint of peach. Simmering the mix for a few minutes blends the flavours and also cooks off some of the alcohol, which helps the lollies freeze.

• •

400ml rosé wine, such as Zinfandel
200ml white grape juice
75g caster sugar
2 peaches
60ml peach schnapps

• •

Pour the wine and grape juice into a medium saucepan and add the sugar. Set the pan on a medium heat and bring to a gentle boil, stirring to dissolve the sugar. When the pan is just bubbling, turn the heat down and simmer for 5 minutes. Pour the mixture into a jug and set aside for 1–2 hours to cool (see the tip on page 16 on using ice baths to cool your lolly mixes quickly).

When you're ready to freeze the ice pops, halve the peaches and scoop out the stones. Slice the fruit into wedges and drop them into the moulds. Stir the peach schnapps into the rosé wine mixture, then pour the mix into moulds and freeze for 2–3 hours until slushy and semi-frozen. Insert sticks into the moulds and freeze overnight until solid.

RUM &
BANANA
ICE POPS

MAKES 6–8

In beach shacks in Jamaica, bartenders shake white rum, coffee liqueur and crème de banane with cream and milk to make Dirty Bananas, the kind of drink that makes you glad you opted for a holiday full of sun, sea, sand and cocktails. Turned into an extravagant ice lolly, the cocktail tastes innocent but it still packs a boozy punch.

200g peeled and sliced bananas
400ml whole milk
75g icing sugar
30ml crème de banane
15ml white rum
15ml coffee liqueur

Tip the bananas into a blender and pour in the milk. Add the sugar, crème de banane, white rum and coffee liqueur. Blitz until smooth and well combined.

Pour the mixture into moulds and freeze for 2–3 hours until slushy and semi-frozen. Insert sticks into the moulds, and freeze overnight until solid.

CHOCOLATE BANANA
FREEZER POPS

MAKES 8

These easy banana pops can be as grown-up or as crazy as you like. Dipped in dark chocolate and sprinkled with chopped hazelnuts and a little sea salt, they're a sophisticated dessert (kind of). Dip the bananas in milk chocolate and coat them with mini marshmallows, caramel shards and pretzel pieces and they're the sort of thing kids – and adults – will go mad for.

● ● ● ● ● ● ● ● ● ● ● ● ● ●   ●

4 bananas
125g dark or milk chocolate
1 tbsp vegetable oil
A few tbsp of toppings, such as sprinkles, desiccated coconut or chopped nuts

*TOP TIP:

For a faster melt, use a microwave set to high and stir every 15 seconds – it's very easy to burn chocolate in a microwave, so watch it carefully.

Line a baking tray with baking paper. Halve the bananas and insert a lolly stick into each half. Lay them on the tray and freeze for 30 minutes.

While the bananas freeze, half-fill a pan with water, set it on a high heat and bring it to a simmer. Snap the chocolate into small pieces and pop them in a heatproof bowl with the vegetable oil. Set the bowl over the pan of water, making sure the bowl doesn't touch the water. Turn the heat off and let the chocolate in the bowl slowly melt, stirring it occasionally. This will take around 20–30 minutes.

Tip any toppings you are going to use into small bowls, so they're easy to reach. Take the semi-frozen bananas out of the freezer. Hold one frozen banana over the bowl of chocolate and spoon over the melted chocolate to lightly coat it. Lay the banana back down on the baking tray and sprinkle over your choice of topping (the chocolate will begin to set straight away, so you need to sprinkle over the toppings as soon as each banana is coated). Repeat to use all the bananas, chocolate and toppings.

Freeze again for around 1 hour, then serve or transfer to a freezerproof tub, layering the lollies with sheets of baking paper. These freezer pops are best eaten within one week of making.

COSMOPOLITAN
PALETAS

MAKES 10

When you're feeling a little Carrie Bradshaw and want to recreate late 90s New York in your kitchen, whip up a batch of these cool and crunchy ice lollies. Based on *Sex and the City*'s signature cocktail, they're a stylish mix of tart cranberry juice, smooth vodka and an orange-scented splash of triple sec. They're the fashion-forward frozen treat of the summer.

250ml Simple Syrup
  (see page 19)
500ml cranberry juice
40ml good-quality vodka
20ml triple sec
Juice of ½ lime
A few dashes of Angostura
  bitters

Make the Simple Syrup following the recipe on page 19, then let it cool.

Pour the cranberry juice into a jug and add the Simple Syrup, vodka, triple sec, lime juice and a few dashes of Angostura bitters (4–5 good shakes should do it). Stir to mix, then pour the cranberry mixture into the moulds.

Freeze for 2–3 hours until semi-frozen. Insert the sticks into the slushy lollies and freeze overnight until solid.

LIME DAIQUIRI
FREEZER POPS

A daiquiri is a Cuban cocktail made with white rum,
lime juice and a touch of sugar. This deep-freezer version adds
buttermilk into the mix to create smooth, creamy lollies with
a tangy edge.

● ● ● ● ● ● ● ● ● ● ● ● ● ●   ●

200ml Simple Syrup
(see page 19)
100ml fresh lime juice
300ml buttermilk
60ml white rum
A few drops of green food
colouring (optional)

Make the Simple Syrup following the recipe on
page 19, then let it cool.

When you're ready to make the lollies, measure out
the Simple Syrup, then add the lime juice, buttermilk
and white rum. Stir to combine. If you want to make
the lollies green, add a few drops of food colouring
and stir it in. Pour the mixture into moulds and freeze
for 2–3 hours until semi-frozen. Insert sticks into the
semi-frozen lollies and freeze overnight until set.

CREAMY MINT CHOC CHIP ICE POPS

MAKES 10

Sweetened condensed milk is your secret weapon when you want to make indulgent ice lollies that have all the richness and velvety texture of ice cream, but without the churning. The basic mix takes just a few minutes to make, and it's very adaptable. I've gone for mint choc chip, as it's my favourite flavour, but you can play around with different combinations. Try vanilla extract and fudge chunks, malted milk powder and crumbled honeycomb, or cocoa powder and chopped, salted peanuts.

75g milk chocolate
397g can sweetened condensed milk
250ml double cream
250ml whole milk
30ml crème de menthe
A few drops of green food colouring (optional)

Grate the chocolate and set it aside for later. Pour the condensed milk and double cream into a mixing bowl and whisk together until smooth. Whisk in the milk. Add the crème de menthe and a few drops of green food colouring, if using, then whisk again briefly to combine. Add the grated chocolate and stir to mix. Use a small ladle to pour the mixture into moulds, or transfer the mix to a jug and pour it in. Freeze for 2–3 hours until semi-frozen. Insert sticks, then freeze overnight until solid.

TIRAMISÚ
PICK-ME-UPS

MAKES 10

In a restaurant in northern Italy in the 1960s, a pastry chef layered up sponge fingers, mascarpone, cream and a dusting of cocoa powder and he called it tiramisú. The name translates from Italian as 'pick me up', and the pudding does indeed perk up anyone who eats it. Not just because of the coffee, or the cheering effects of a bowlful of cream and chocolate, but because tiramisú is said to be an aphrodisiac. I can't promise these portable tiramisús will win over the object of your affection, but they will definitely be impressed by your lolly-making skills, which has to count for something, right?

● ● ● ● ● ● ● ● ● ● ● ● ●

25g dark chocolate
125g mascarpone
397g can sweetened
  condensed milk
350ml double cream
1 tsp. unsweetened cocoa
  powder
30ml espresso, cooled
30ml coffee liqueur
1 tsp. vanilla extract
30ml brandy
10 sponge fingers

● ●

Coarsely grate the chocolate and set aside. Spoon the mascarpone into a mixing bowl and beat until smooth and creamy. Slowly whisk in the condensed milk until it is evenly combined, then add the cream and whisk that in, too. Ladle half the mix out into a separate bowl. Add the cocoa powder, the espresso and the coffee liqueur to one of the bowls and whisk them together. Stir in half the grated chocolate.
To the other bowl, add the vanilla extract and the brandy. Whisk to combine. Cover the vanilla mixture and store it in your fridge for later.

Use a small ladle to pour the chocolatey mixture into the moulds to half-fill them – these lollies are best made in rigid plastic moulds – or transfer the mix to a jug to pour in. Break up a sponge finger and stir through in each mould. Pop the lollies into the freezer for 2–3 hours until semi-frozen.

Take the moulds out of the freezer and spoon in the vanilla mix to fill them. Sprinkle the remaining grated chocolate over the ice pops. Insert the sticks and freeze overnight until solid.

SPICED WHISKY & FIG CREAM POPS

MAKES 8

This ice pop was inspired by masala chai, the sweet, spicy tea that keeps India running. You need to allow a few hours to infuse the sweetened milk with the spices, and when you're picking a whisky, go for one that is more nutty and biscuity than smoky.

397g can sweetened
  condensed milk
400ml whole milk
4 green cardamom pods
1 star anise
8 cloves
½ tsp. black peppercorns
A slice of fresh ginger
60ml good-quality whisky
2 figs
8 cinnamon sticks
  (optional)

Pour the condensed milk into a saucepan. Add the milk and whisk together until smooth. Press the cardamom pods with the flat of a knife to crack them open a little. Add them to the pan with the star anise, cloves, peppercorns and ginger. Put the pan on a medium heat and bring to the boil, stirring to stop the mix sticking and burning. Once the pan starts to bubble, take it off the heat and set aside for 2 hours to cool and infuse.

When you're ready to make the ice pops, strain the milk mixture through a sieve into a jug. Stir in the whisky. Slice the figs into 4 slices each and pop them in the moulds. Pour in the mixture and freeze for 2–3 hours until semi-frozen. Insert cinnamon sticks into the slushy lollies, if you're using them, or wooden sticks. Return to the freezer and freeze overnight until solid.

PIÑA COLADA ICE POPS

MAKES 10–12

If you like piña coladas, you'll make these ice lollies again and again. They're rich and fruity, thanks to the mix of coconut and pineapple, which also gives them a soft, fluffy texture.

• •

100ml Simple Syrup (see page 19)
430g can pineapple chunks in juice
400ml can coconut milk
60ml white rum
Juice of ½ lime
25g coconut cream

• •

Make the Simple Syrup following the recipe on page 19 then let it cool.

Tip the can of pineapple and its juice into a blender. Pour in the coconut milk, Simple Syrup, white rum and lime juice. Crumble in the coconut cream and blitz until combined. Pour the mixture into moulds and freeze for 2–3 hours until semi-frozen. Insert sticks and freeze overnight until solid.

RASPBERRY & COCONUT PUNCH POPS

MAKES 6–8

Raspberries and coconut don't get paired up enough. They're a dynamic duo, especially in desserts. These lollies have a rich coconut base topped with a vodka-spiked raspberry purée that freezes into a mouthwatering treat.

150ml Simple Syrup
  (see page 19)
250g raspberries
Juice of ½ lime
60ml good-quality vodka
200ml coconut milk

Make the Simple Syrup following the recipe on page 19, then let it cool.

Tip the raspberries into a blender. Add 75ml of the Simple Syrup, along with the lime juice and vodka, and blitz until smooth. Pour the mixture into moulds. Freeze for 2–3 hours until semi-frozen. Pour the coconut milk into a bowl and add the remaining Simple Syrup to it. Whisk together and pour the coconut mixture into the moulds. Insert the sticks and freeze overnight until solid.

FRANGELICO & CHOCOLATE POPS

MAKES 10

Full of toasted hazelnuts and sweet vanilla, Frangelico is as good poured over a bowl of ice cream as it is served in a glass over ice. Add it to a fudgy chocolate ice lolly and you get an extra boost of smoky cocoa flavour. No Frangelico? Use Amaretto instead, and decorate your lollies with toasted flaked almonds.

● ● ● ● ● ● ● ● ● ● ● ● ● ● ● ●

50g icing sugar
2 heaped tbsp. unsweetened cocoa powder
300ml whole milk
300ml single cream
60ml Frangelico liqueur
1 tsp. vanilla extract
A pinch of flaky sea salt
Chopped toasted hazelnuts, to serve

● ●

Tip the icing sugar and cocoa powder into a mixing bowl and add a splash of milk. Whisk together to make a smooth paste. Add a splash more milk and whisk again. Keep going until you have added all the milk and everything is smoothly combined. Pour in the cream, Frangelico and vanilla extract, add a pinch of salt and whisk together briefly until combined. Pour into moulds, freeze for 2–3 hours, then insert sticks and freeze overnight until solid.

To serve, unmould the lollies and sprinkle with a few chopped toasted hazelnuts. You can refreeze the lollies once you've added the hazelnuts, to set them (see the tip on page 17 on setting and storing your lollies).

KIWI CAIPIRINHA COOLERS

MAKES 8–10

Take your freezer on a trip to Brazil with these lollies inspired by the famous Latin American drink. The cocktail itself is a simple mix of lime, sugar and cachaça – a spirit made from sugar cane. To make a longer drink suitable for freezing, I've upped the lime juice and added tart kiwi fruits. If you don't have any cachaça, use white rum instead.

〰〰〰〰〰〰〰〰　　〰〰〰〰〰〰〰〰〰

350ml Simple Syrup
  (see page 19)
2 kiwi fruits
200ml fresh lime juice
150ml cold water
60ml cachaça

Make the Simple Syrup following the recipe on page 19, then let it cool.

Slice the skin off the kiwis and pop them in a blender. Add the Simple Syrup, lime juice and water and blitz until smooth. If you'd like clear lollies, pour the mixture through a sieve into a jug to catch any unblended seeds or pulp. Don't press the pulp to squeeze out any remaining juice – that will make the lollies cloudy. Stir in the cachaça.

Pour the mixture into moulds. Freeze for 2–3 hours until semi-frozen. Insert sticks into the slushy lollies and freeze overnight until solid.

MELON MOJITO FREEZER POPS

A simple mix of mint, lime and sugar muddled with rum, cooling mojitos have been drunk in Cuba for over 100 years. The final ingredient in the cocktail is soda water, but you need something sweeter to carry the flavours in an ice lolly. Galia melon, lush and fragrant, is the perfect stand-in.

• •

450g chopped Galia melon
2 tbsp. caster sugar
2 sprigs fresh mint, leaves only
Juice of 1 lime
60ml white rum

• •

Tip the melon into a blender. Add the sugar, mint leaves, lime juice and white rum. Blitz until blended and smooth. Pour the mixture into moulds and freeze for 2–3 hours until semi-frozen. Insert sticks into the moulds and freeze overnight until set.

WATERMELON MARGARITA PALETAS

MAKES 6

Paleterías in Mexico specialise in *paletas* (ice lollies) made from fresh, seasonal ingredients. I have followed their lead and kept these ice pops simple: plenty of juicy watermelon, a squeeze of lime to bring out the flavour and a touch of sugar. You don't have to turn these *paletas* into margaritas – they're great eaten just as they are –but they are fun served in glasses with a shot of tequila and triple sec. You can decide just how much watermelon you want melted in your ice-cold margarita.

450g chopped watermelon
Juice of 2 limes
2 tbsp caster sugar
Lime or lemon juice, flaky sea salt, chilled silver tequila and triple sec, and halved jalapeños, to serve

Flick as many of the black seeds out of the watermelon as possible, then tip the chunks of fruit into a blender. Add the lime juice and sugar. Blitz to make a smooth purée. For clear paletas, pour the purée through a sieve into a jug to catch any unblended seeds or pulp. Don't press the fruit in the sieve to extract more juice – that will make the paletas cloudy. Pour the watermelon mixture into moulds and freeze for 2–3 hours until slushy and semi-frozen. Insert the wooden sticks into the moulds, and freeze overnight until set.

To serve the paletas as a poptail, prepare a glass for every guest. Dip the rims of wide tumblers in lime or lemon juice and then in flaky sea salt to lightly coat. Add 30ml chilled silver tequila and 30ml chilled triple sec to each glass and stir to mix. Add a watermelon paleta to each glass and tuck in a jalapeño. Let it sit for 2–3 minutes to begin melting into the drink, then serve.

MERRY BERRY MULLED WINE ICE POPS

MAKES 8

Looking for a lolly for Christmas? Look no further. Mulled wine, full of sugar and spice, is great frozen – especially if you stir in some crushed berries. Choose a juicy red wine, like Merlot, Shiraz or Gamay, and if you don't like the spices I've suggested, add your own mix. Cardamom pods, peppercorns, fennel seeds, cloves or strips of orange or lemon peel would all work really well.

400ml fruity red wine
200ml fresh orange juice
75g caster sugar
1 cinnamon stick
1 star anise
A couple of slices of fresh ginger
110g mixed berries, defrosted if frozen

Pour the wine and orange juice into a medium saucepan and add the sugar, cinnamon, star anise and fresh ginger. Set the pan on a medium heat and bring to a gentle boil, stirring to dissolve the sugar. When the liquid is just bubbling, turn the heat down and simmer for 5 minutes. Set aside for 1–2 hours to cool (see the tip on page 16 on using ice baths to cool your lolly mixes quickly).

When you're ready to freeze the ice lollies, place the mixed berries into a bowl and use a fork to roughly crush them. Strain the mulled wine into the bowl with the berries and stir to mix. Ladle the mix into moulds and freeze for 2–3 hours until semi-frozen. Insert sticks into the moulds and freeze overnight until solid.

INDEX

CREDITS

All images courtesy of Shutterstock.

The author would like to thank her mum and dad for letting her turn their kitchen into an ice-lolly factory. And also all their neighbours, who gamely agreed to eat the ice lollies and may have got more ice pops packed into their freezers than they bargained for.